ORIGAMI

HIDEAKI SAKATA

Published by Japan Publications Trading Co., Ltd.,
1-2-1 Sarugaku-cho, Chiyoda-ku, Tokyo, 101 Japan

Designed and illustrated by Annu Shizawa
First edition, First printing: October 1997

Distributors:
United States: Kodansha America, Inc. through Oxford University Press,
   198 Madison Avenue, New York, NY 10016.
Canada: Fitzhenry & Whiteside Ltd.,
   195 Allstate Parkway, Markham, Ontario L3R 4T8.
United Kingdom and Europe: Premier Book Marketing Ltd.,
   1 Gower Street, London WC1E 6HA.
Australia and New Zealand: Bookwise International,
   54 Crittenden Road, Findon, South Australia 5023.
The Far East and Japan: Japan Publications Trading Co., Ltd.,
   1-2-1 Sarugaku-cho, Chiyoda-ku, Tokyo, 101 Japan.

10 9 8 7 6 5 4 3 2 1

ISBN 0-87040-999-9

Printed in Japan

CONTENTS

"PUPPETS"

"CUP and DISH"

Folding Symbols Used in this book

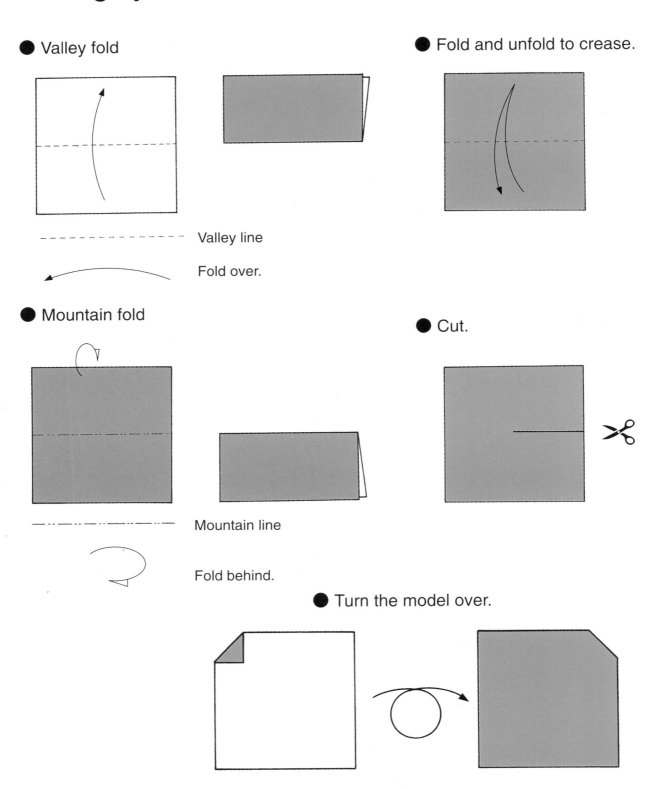

● Valley fold

- - - - - - - - - - -   Valley line

Fold over.

● Fold and unfold to crease.

● Mountain fold

·— · — · — · — · —   Mountain line

Fold behind.

● Cut.

● Turn the model over.

● Open and flatten.

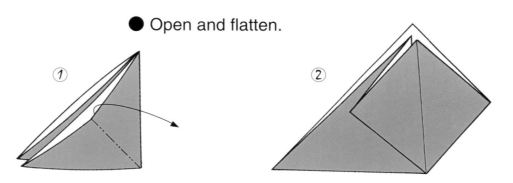

Bring top layer corner up
and flatten to make a square.

● Enlarged

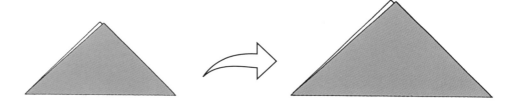

● Pocket fold

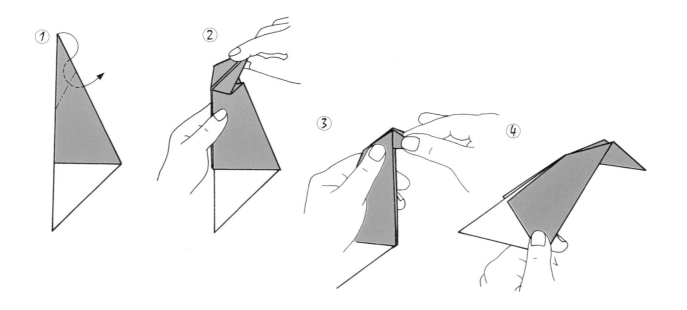

PUPPETS

①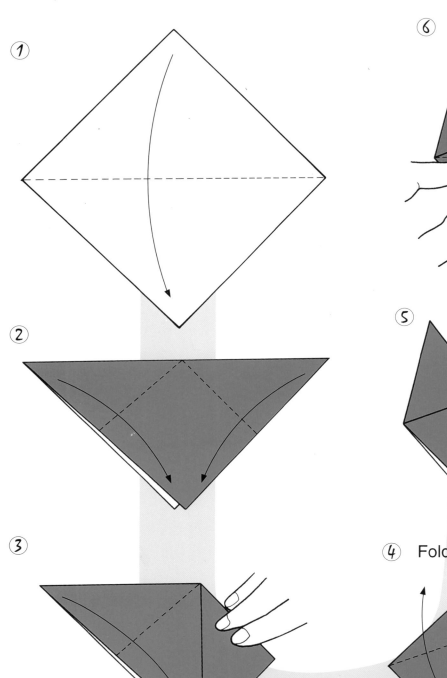

②

③

④ Fold up along the lines.

⑤

⑥ Fold the top layer up.

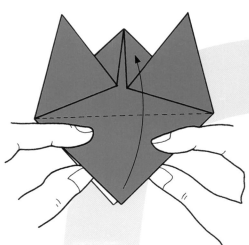

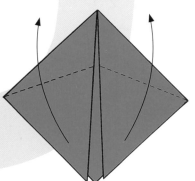

⑦

⑧ Fold both sides along the lines.

⑨

Turn the model over.

⑩

Draw the face.

COMPLETE Kitten

⑪

COMPLETE Puppy

⑫

Fold the ears down.

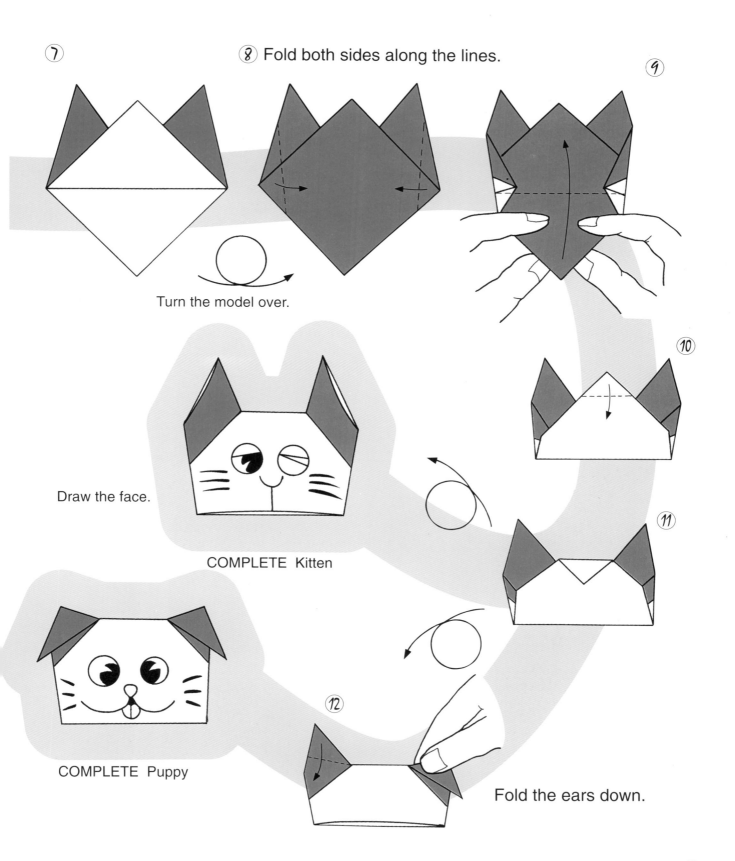

7

AIRPLANE

Use a rectangular paper.

① Fold and unfold to crease.

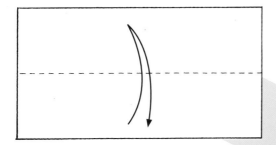

②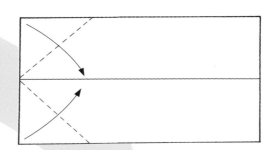

③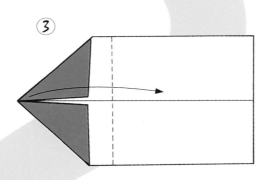

Enlarged.

④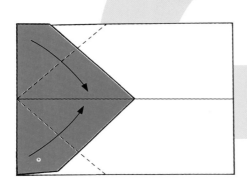

⑤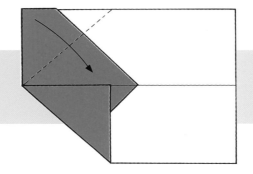

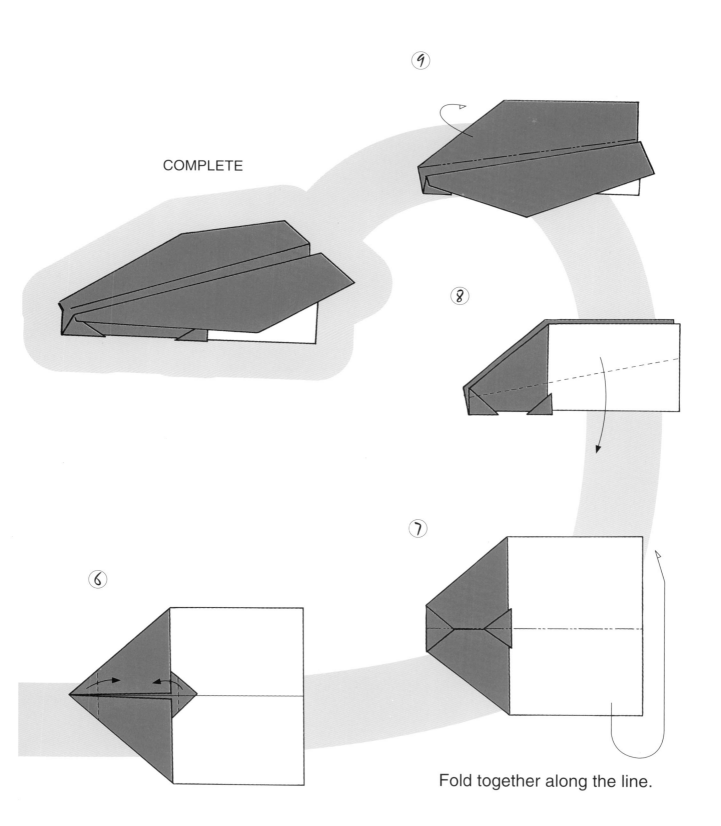

COMPLETE

⑨

⑧

⑦

⑥

Fold together along the line.

SNAPPER

Use a rectangular paper.

① Fold and unfold to crease.

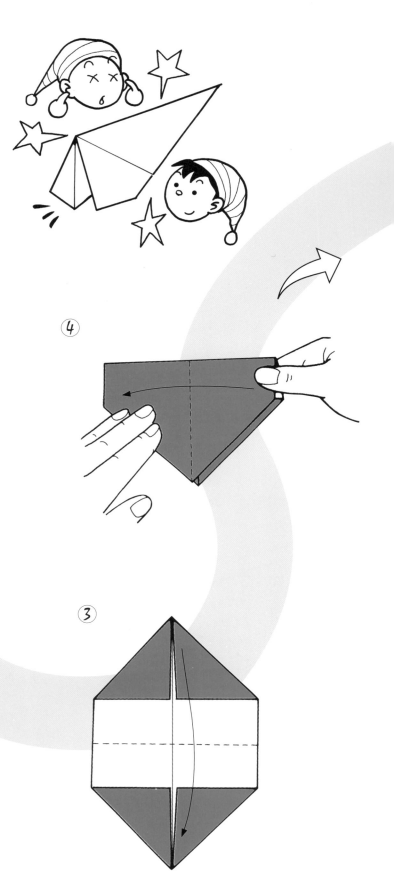

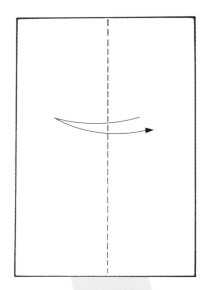

②

③

④

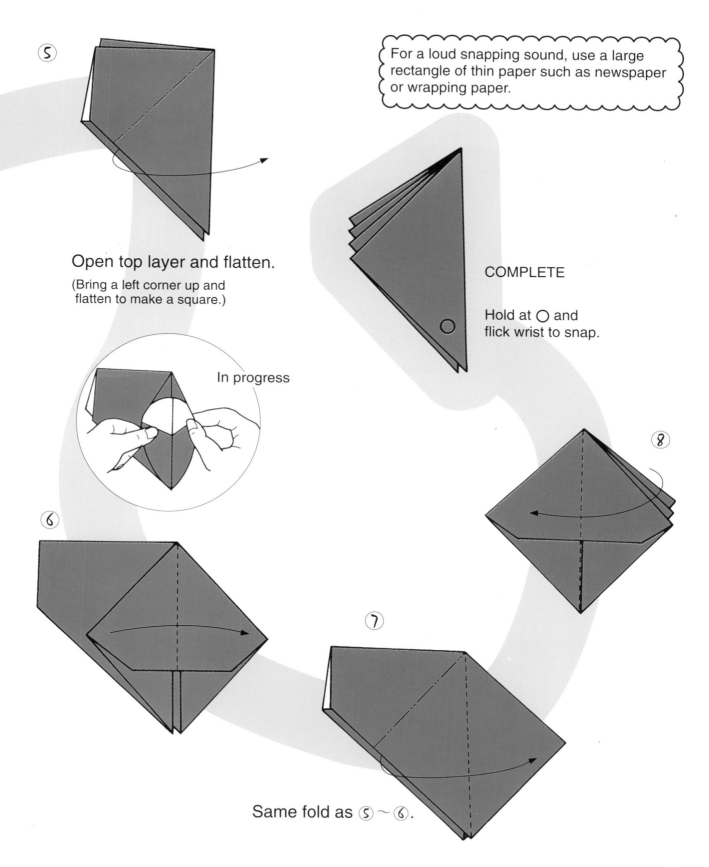

⑤

Open top layer and flatten.
(Bring a left corner up and
flatten to make a square.)

In progress

For a loud snapping sound, use a large
rectangle of thin paper such as newspaper
or wrapping paper.

COMPLETE

Hold at ○ and
flick wrist to snap.

⑥

⑦

⑧

Same fold as ⑤〜⑥.

PIANO

①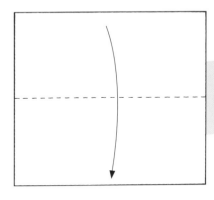

Fold and unfold to crease.

②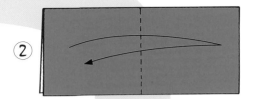

③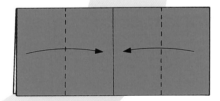

④ Fold the top layer back and flatten.

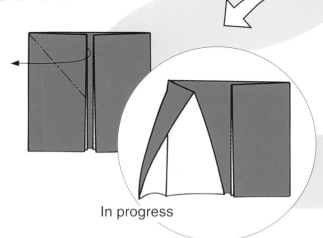

In progress

⑤ Same as other side.

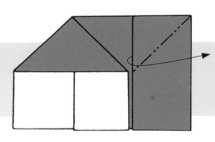

⑨ Bring the keyboard down.

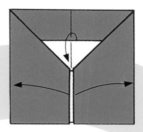

COMPLETE

Open top layers to both sides.

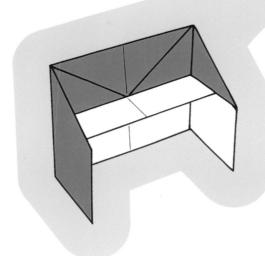

⑧

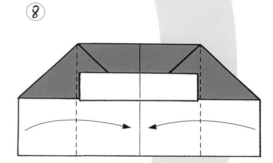

⑦

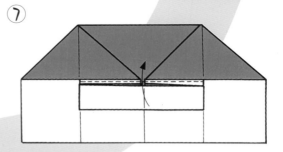

⑥ Fold up along the line.

Fold up again along the line.

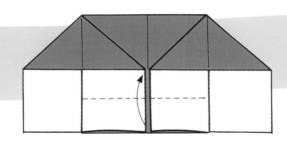

TRUCK

BODY

① Fold and unfold to crease.

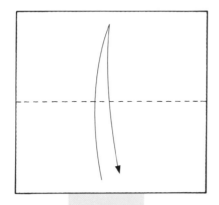

COMPLETE

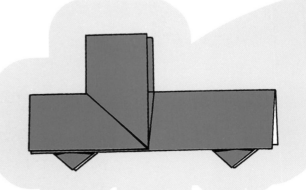

Set the driver's seat on the body, and glue.

②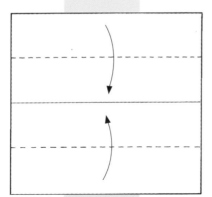

Body

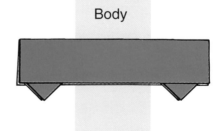

③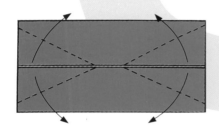

Fold top layers up along the lines.

④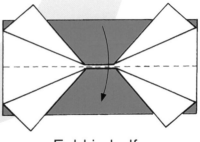

Fold in half.

Driver's seat

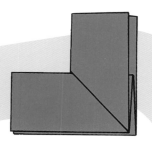

DRIVER'S SEAT

① Fold and unfold to crease.

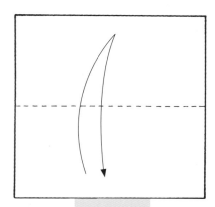

②

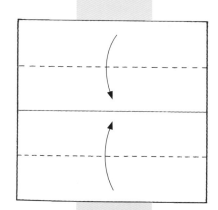

③

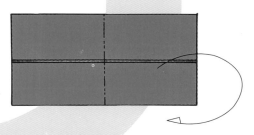

Mountain fold

⑦
Mountain fold

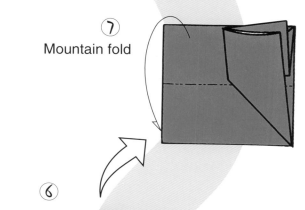

⑥

Match the two dots
of the top layer.

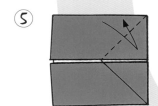

⑤

Repeat as same as ④.

④

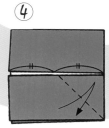

Fold top layer and
unfold to crease.

JET AIRPLANE

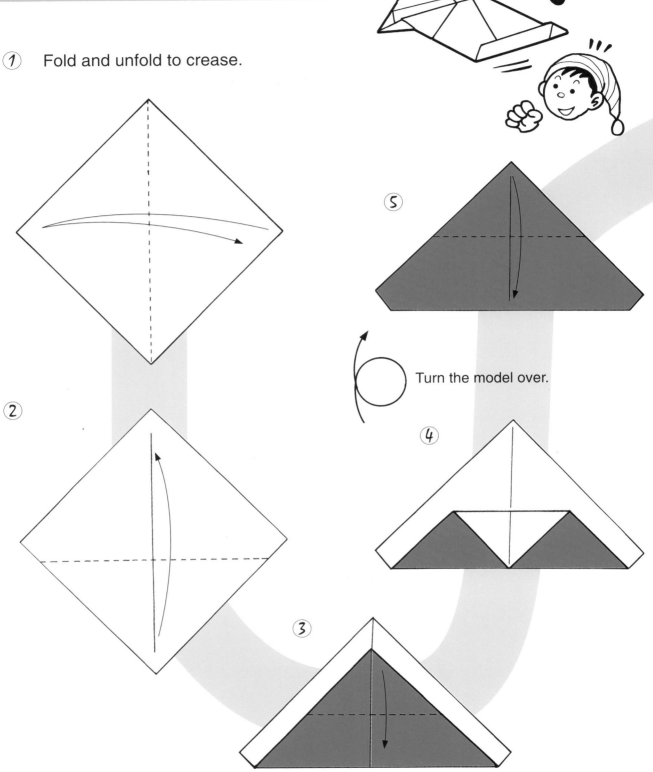

① Fold and unfold to crease.

②

③

④

⑤

Turn the model over.

⑥

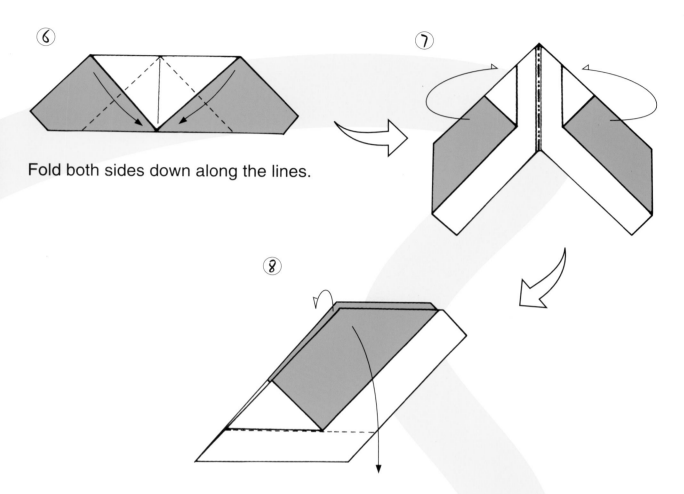

Fold both sides down along the lines.

⑦

⑧

Fold both sides down along the lines.

COMPLETE

⑨

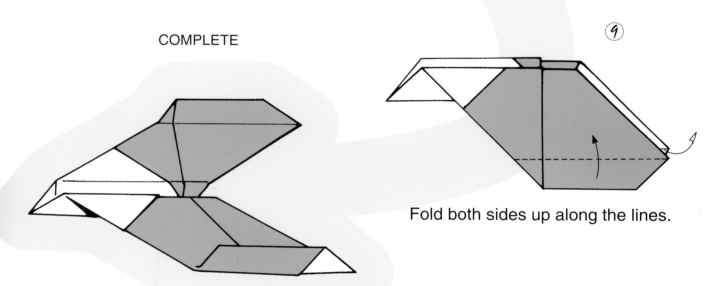

Fold both sides up along the lines.

RABBIT

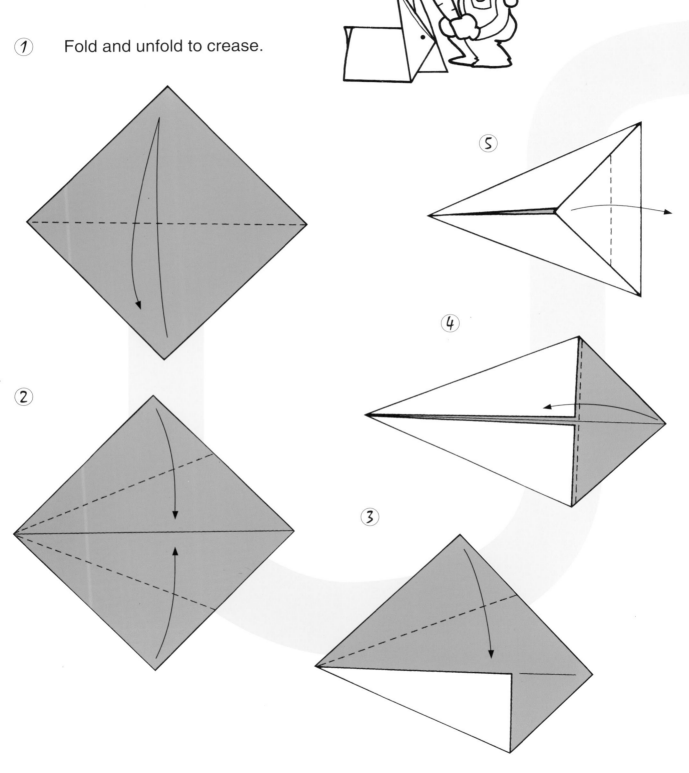

① Fold and unfold to crease.

②

③

④

⑤

⑥ Cut.

⑦ Fold down along the line.

COMPLETE

Draw the eyes.

⑧

⑨

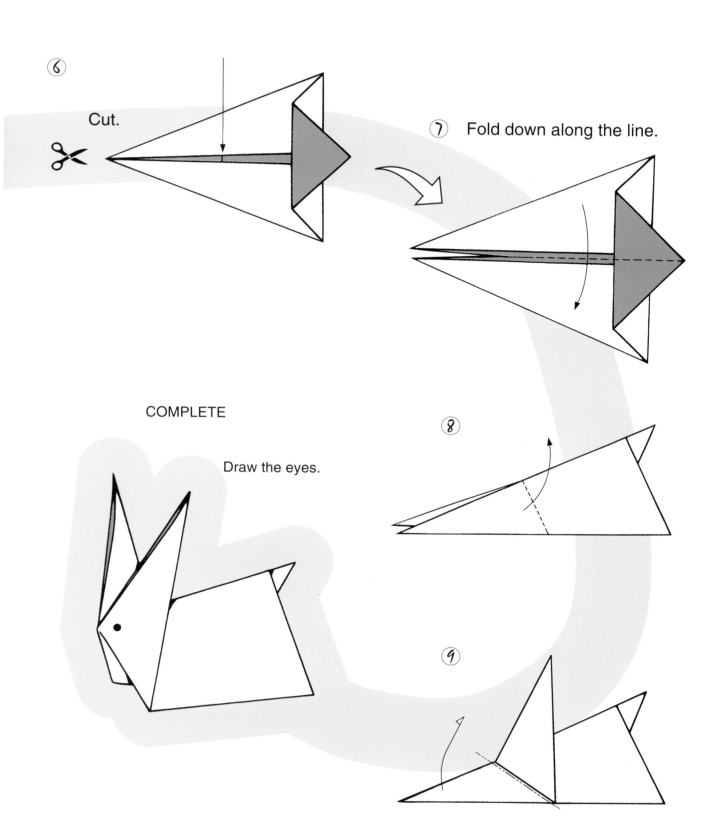

MONKEY

①

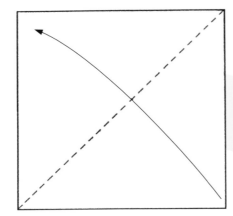

②

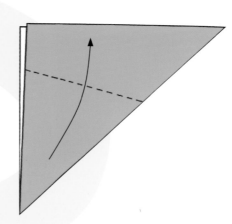

③

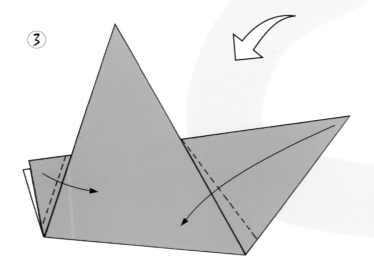

④

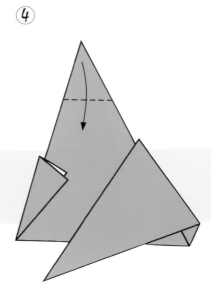

20

COMPLETE

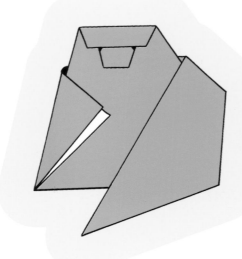

⑦

Mountain
fold

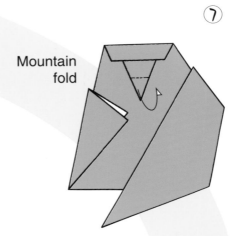

⑥

⑤ Fold down again along the line.

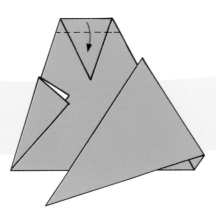

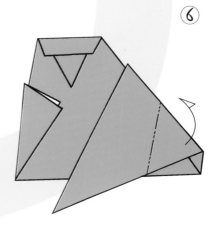

Mountain fold along the line.

TORTOISE

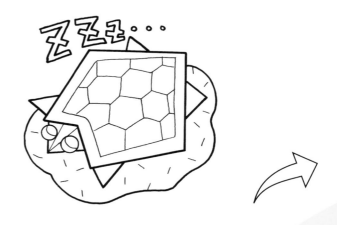

Make a center line.

① Fold and unfold to crease.

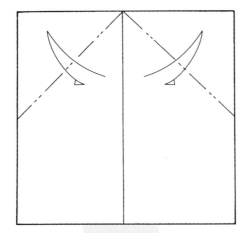

②

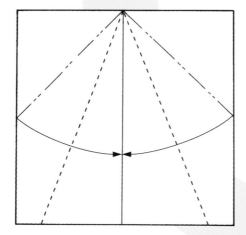

Fold both sides along the center line.

④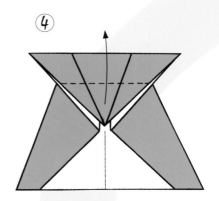

Fold top layer along the line.

③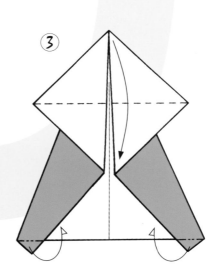

5 Fold both sides along the center line.

6

7

COMPLETE

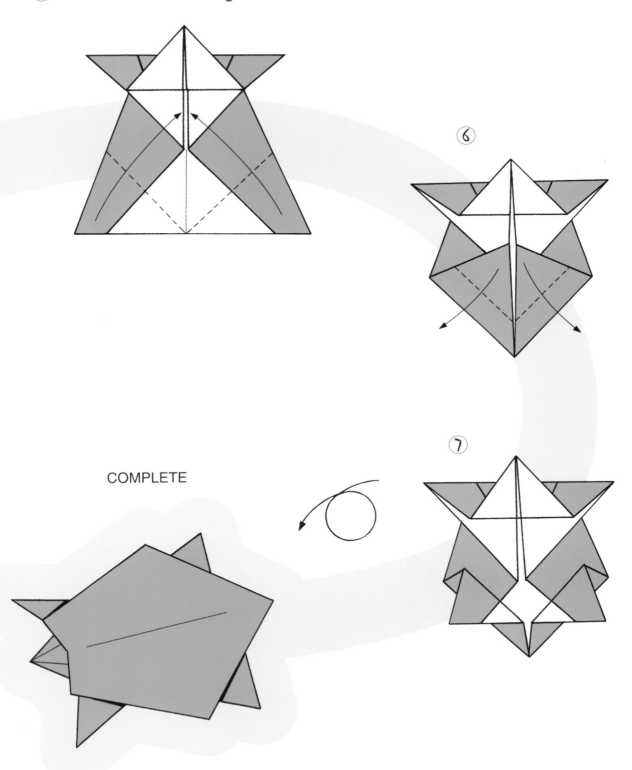

BUTTERFLY

①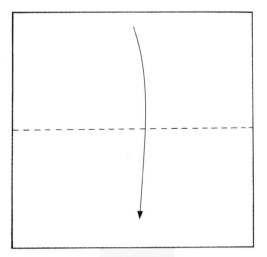

②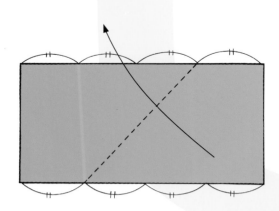

③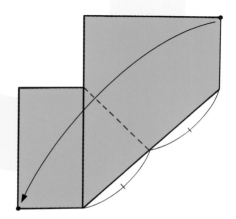

④ Fold top layer along the line.

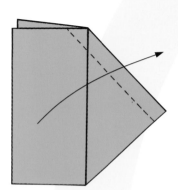

⑤

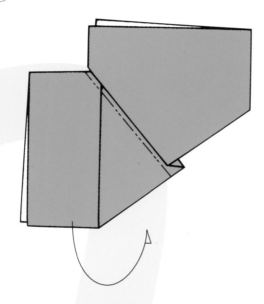

Mountain fold along the line.

⑥ Open both sides.

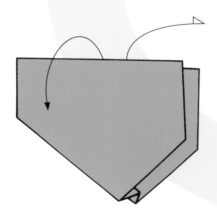

COMPLETE

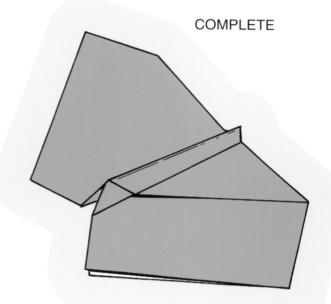

⑦

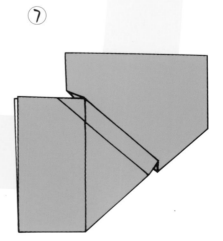

LIGHTNING BUG

①

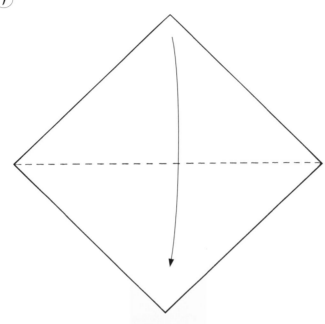

②

③ Fold to the center.

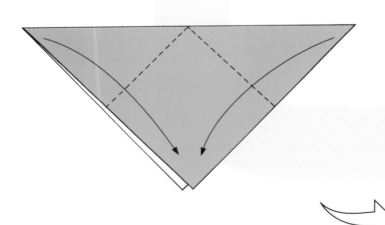

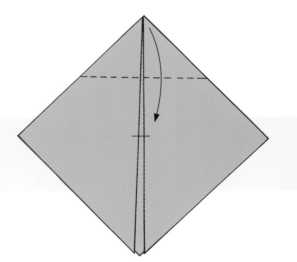

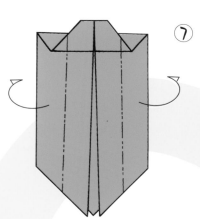

7 Mountain fold both sides along the lines.

COMPLETE

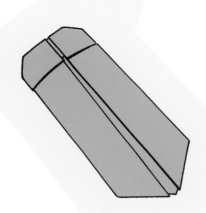

6 Mountain fold both sides along the lines.

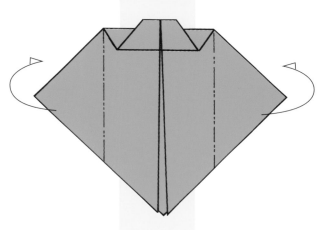

4

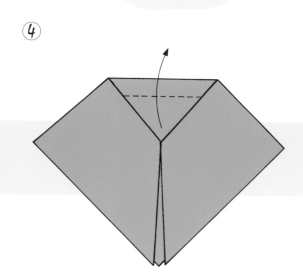

5

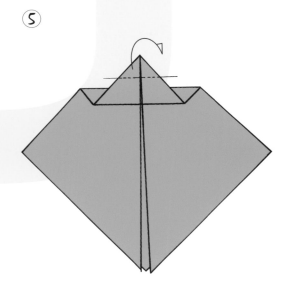

FLOWER and LEAF

FLOWER

Fold both sides to the center line.
Same as other sides.

①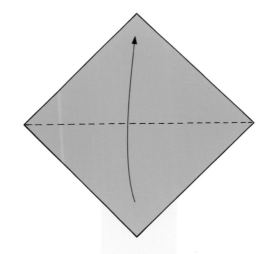

②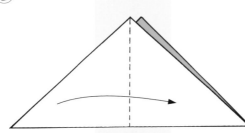

③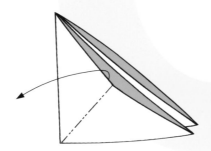

Bring the left corner up
and flatten to make a square.

④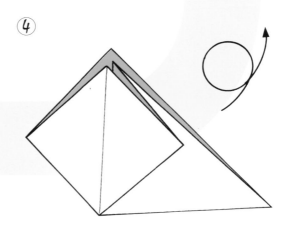

⑤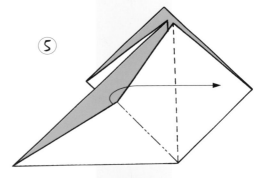

Bring the right corner up
and flatten to make a square.

⑥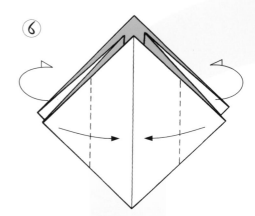

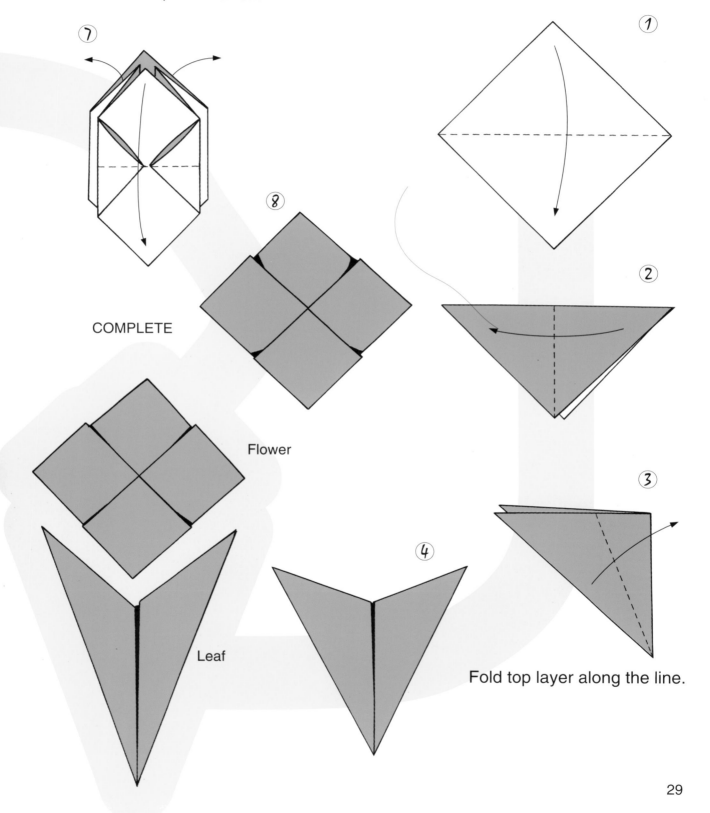

Fold top layer half way down along the line and pull out other sides, and flatten.

LEAF

⑦

⑧

COMPLETE

Flower

Leaf

①

②

③

④

Fold top layer along the line.

29

ROSE

Fold and unfold to crease.

1

2

3

4

5

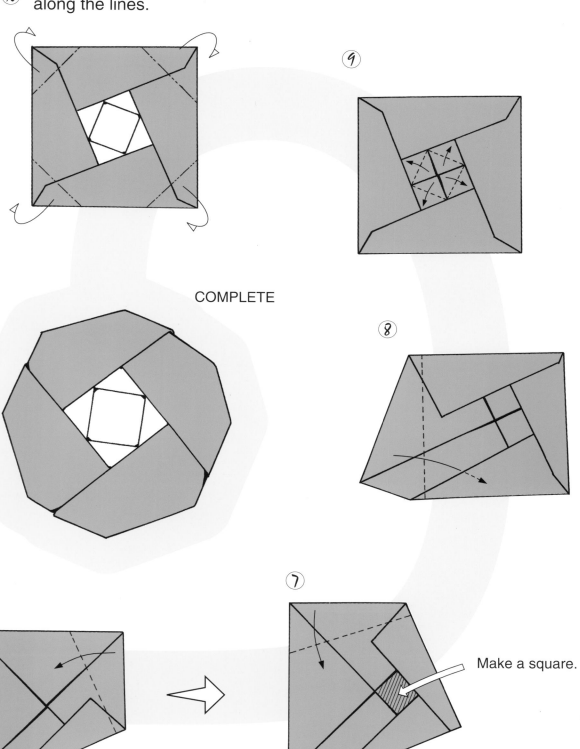

⑩ Mountain fold all corners along the lines.

⑨

COMPLETE

⑧

⑥

⑦

Make a square.

PANSY

①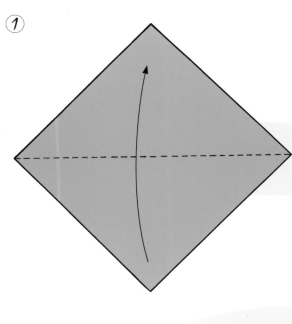

②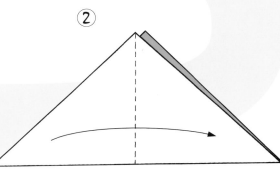

③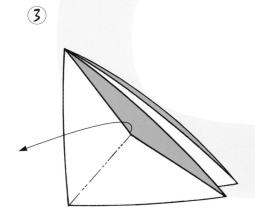

Bring top layer up and
flatten to make a square.

④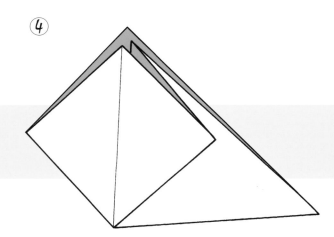

⑦ Fold top layer along the line and open the other layers.

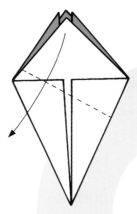

⑧ Mountain fold three corners along the lines.

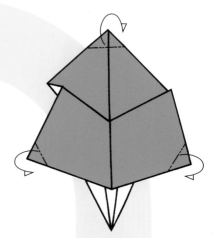

⑥ Fold along the center line. Do same on other side.

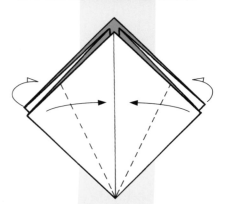

⑤

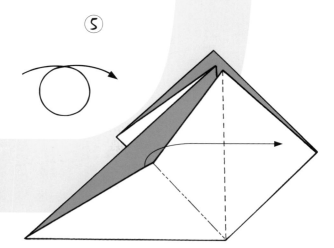

Repeat as same as ③~④.

COMPLETE

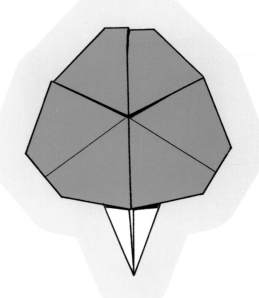

BOX

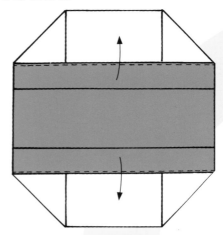

1 × 2 rectangular paper.

① Make a center line
and fold along the center line.

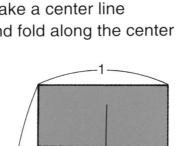

②

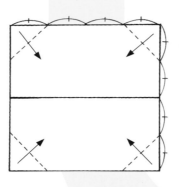

④ Fold both sides again along
the lines.

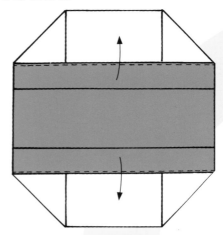

③ Fold the top layer of both sides
along the lines.

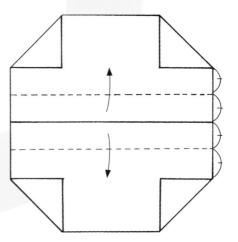

(5) Fold to the center.

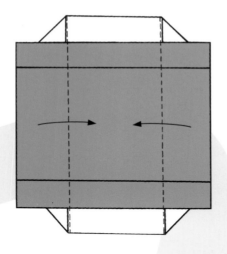

COMPLETE

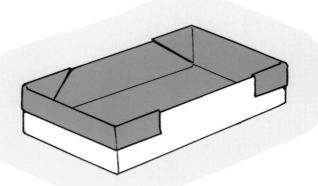

(6)

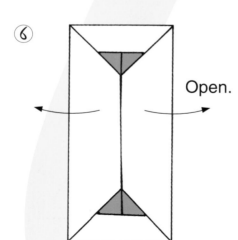

Open.

(7) Open both sides.

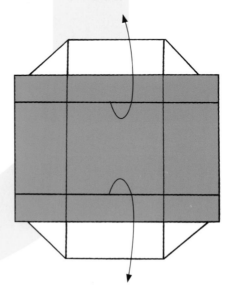

CUP and DISH

CUP

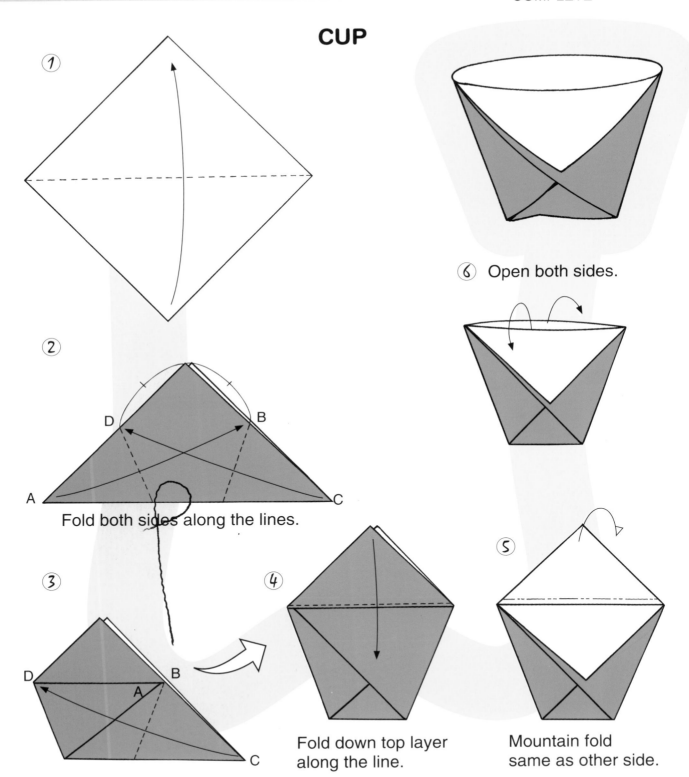

①

② D B A C
Fold both sides along the lines.

③ D B A C

④ Fold down top layer along the line.

⑤ Mountain fold same as other side.

⑥ Open both sides.

36

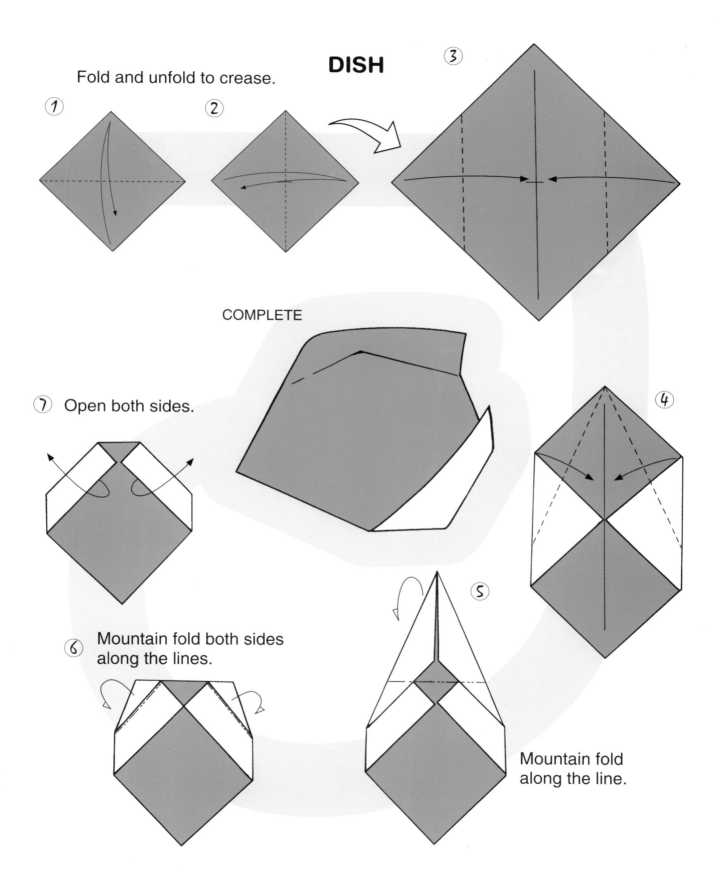

DISH

Fold and unfold to crease.

① ② ③

COMPLETE

⑦ Open both sides.

④

⑤

⑥ Mountain fold both sides along the lines.

Mountain fold along the line.

PURSE and CAP

①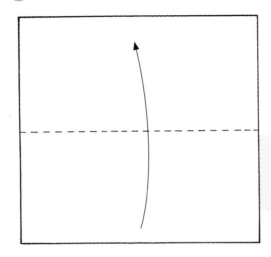

② Fold along the center line.

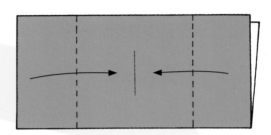

③ Bring top layer corner up along the line and flatten.

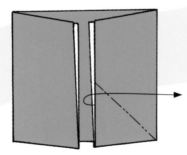

④ Same as other side.

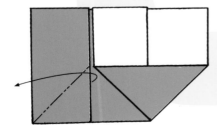

⑤ Mountain fold both sides along the lines.

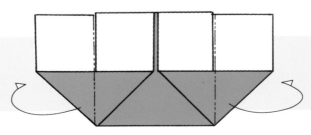

COMPLETE Purse

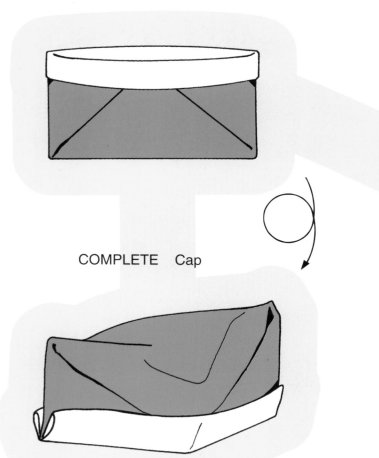

COMPLETE Cap

⑥ Fold over twice.

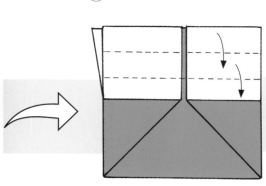

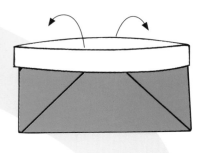

⑧ Fold again.
Same as on the other side.

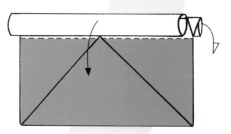

⑦ Same as on the other side.

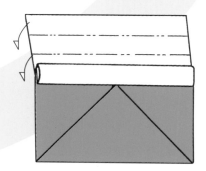

ANGEL FISH

①   Fold and unfold to crease.

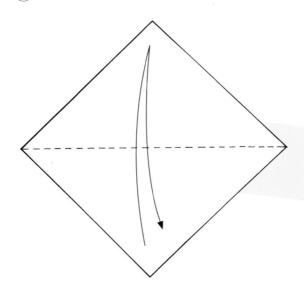

②

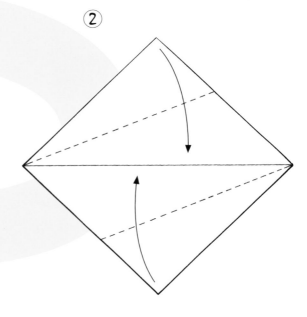

③   Fold both sides again
along the center line.

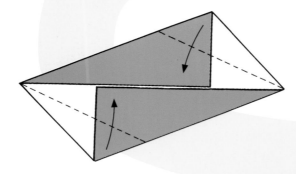

④

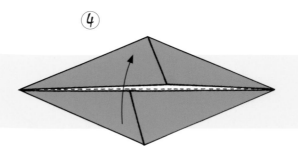

⑦ Join units as in the drawing and glue.

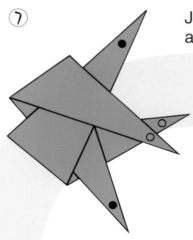

⑥ **Fold one more unit.**
（same fold as steps ① ～ ⑥.）

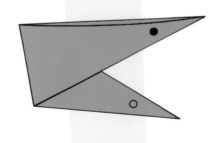

Draw the eyes.

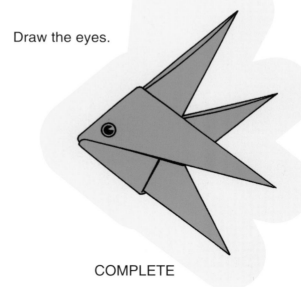

COMPLETE

⑤

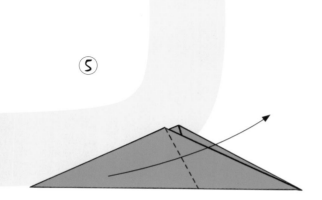

SHARK

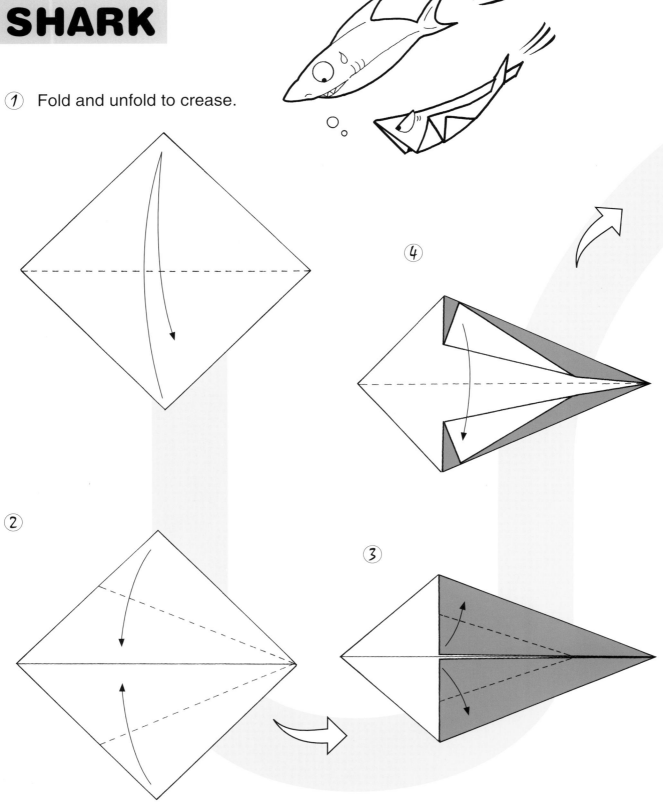

① Fold and unfold to crease.

②

③

④

42

⑤ Fold both sides up along the lines.

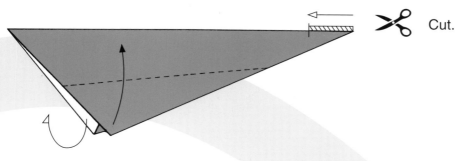

Cut.

⑥ Fold top layer along the line.

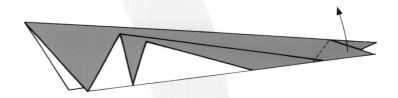

COMPLETE

Draw the eyes.

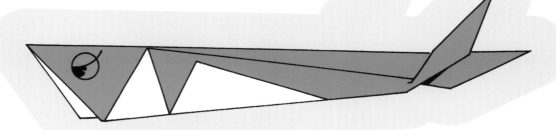

FLATFISH

①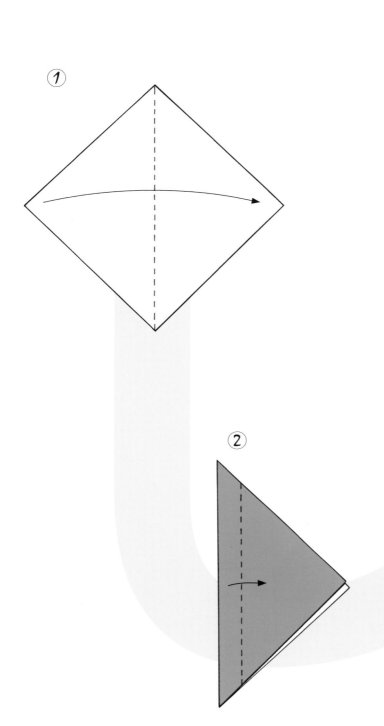

②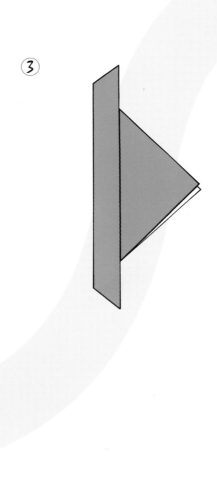

③

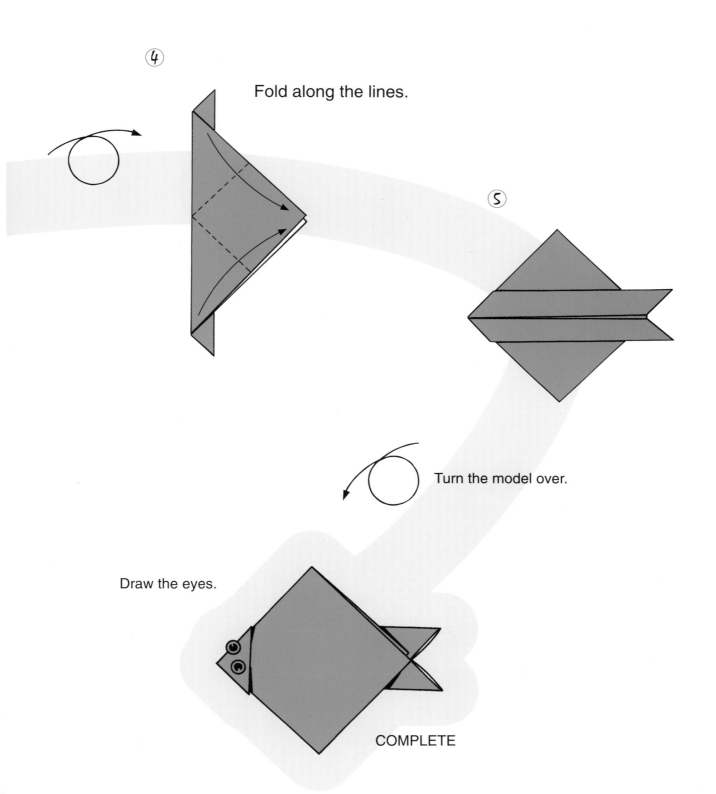

④

Fold along the lines.

⑤

Turn the model over.

Draw the eyes.

COMPLETE

CRANE

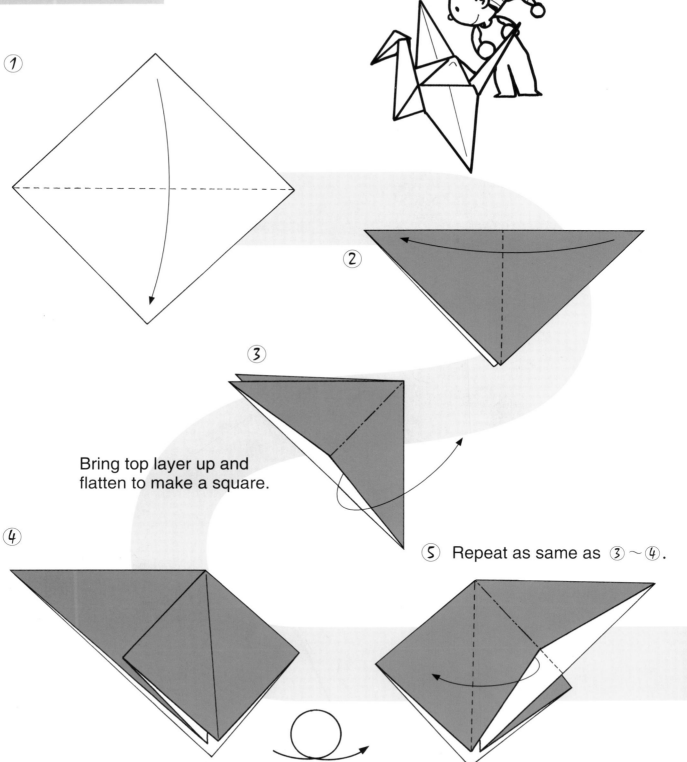

①

②

③ Bring top layer up and flatten to make a square.

④

⑤ Repeat as same as ③ ～ ④.

⑧

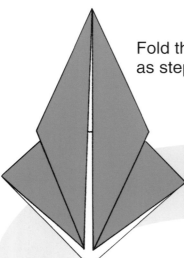

Fold the other side the same
as steps ⑥ ~ ⑧ .

⑨ Fold along the lines.
Same as other side.

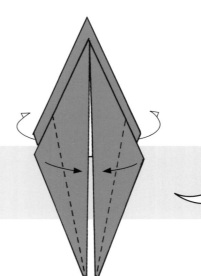

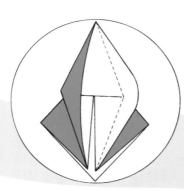

Bring the bottom tip up
and flatten to make a rhombus.

⑦

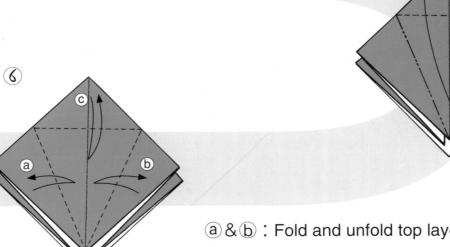

⑥

ⓐ & ⓑ : Fold and unfold top layers to crease.
ⓒ : Fold and unfold to crease.

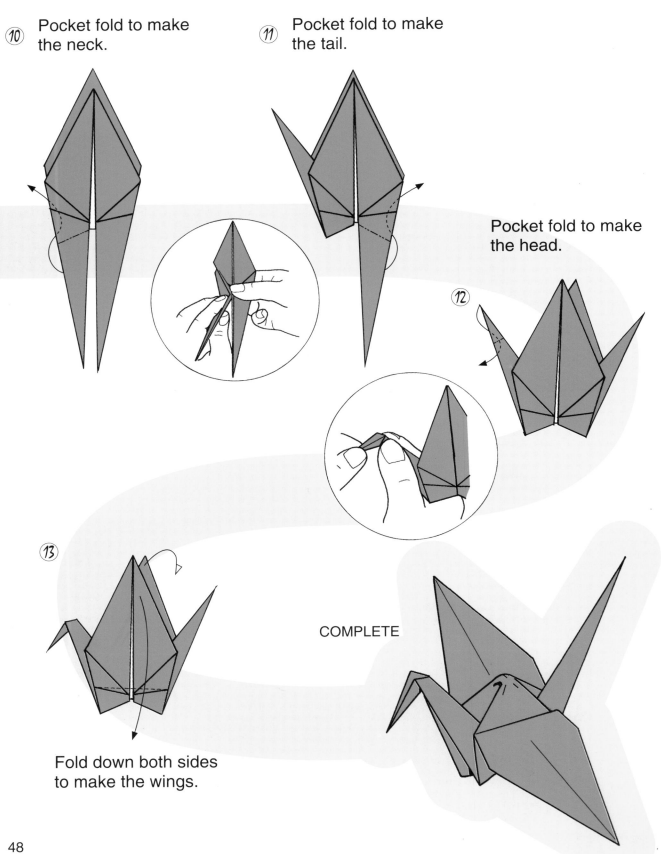

⑩ Pocket fold to make the neck.

⑪ Pocket fold to make the tail.

Pocket fold to make the head.

⑫

⑬

COMPLETE

Fold down both sides to make the wings.

ORIGAMI BOOKS
from Japan Publications

BRILLIANT ORIGAMI: A Collection of Original Designs by David Brill
240 pp., 7 1/4 x 10 1/4 in., 8 pp. color, 215 pp. line drawings, paperback.
ISBN: 0-87040-896-8

COMPLETE ORIGAMI COLLECTION, THE, by Toshie Takahama
160 pp., 7 1/4 x 10 1/4 in., 8 pp. color, 147 pp. line drawings, paperback.
ISBN: 0-87040-960-3

CREATIVE ORIGAMI by Kunihiko Kasahara
180 pp., 8 1/4 x 11 3/4 in., 8 pp. b/w photos, 160 pp. line drawings, paperback.
ISBN: 0-87040-411-3

FLYING BIRD ORIGAMI by Yoshihiko Momotani
70 pp., 7 1/4 x 9 in., 4 pp. color, 62 pp. line drawings, paperback.
ISBN: 0-87040-908-5

HAPPY ORIGAMI: Simple & Easy Origami for Families by Toshie Takahama
Boxed set, board-book: 30 pp., 6 x 6 in., 30 pp. full color, plus origami paper: 6 x 6 in., 70 sheets.
ISBN: 0-87040-986-7

JOYFUL ORIGAMI BOXES, by Tomoko Fuse
96 pp., 7 1/4 x 10 1/4 in., 8 pp. color, 76 pp. two-color illustrations, paperback.
ISBN: 0-87040-974-3

KUSUDAMA: Ball Origami by Makoto Yamaguchi
72 pp., 7 1/4 x 10 1/4 in., 8 pp. color, 65 pp. line drawings, paperback.
ISBN: 0-87040-863-1

MAGIC OF ORIGAMI, THE, by Alice Gray and Kunihiko Kasahara with cooperation of Lillian Oppenheimer and Origami Center of America
132 pp., 7 1/4 x 10 1/4 in., 122 pp. b/w photos and line drawings, paperback.
ISBN: 0-87040-624-8

ORIGAMI by Hideki Sakata
66 pp., 7 1/4 x 10 1/4 in., 66 pp. full color illustrations, paperback.
ISBN: 0-87040-580-2

ORIGAMI ANIMALS by Keiji Kitamura
88 pp., 8 1/4 x 10 1/4 in., 88 pp. full color illustrations, 12 sheets of origami paper included, paperback.
ISBN: 0-87040-941-7

ORIGAMI BOXES by Tomoko Fuse
72 pp., 7 1/4 x 10 1/4 in., 8 pp. color, 60 pp. line drawings, paperback.
ISBN: 0-87040-821-6

ORIGAMI CLASSROOM I by Dokuotei Nakano
Boxed set, board-book: 24 pp., 6 x 6 in., 24 pp. full color illustrations, plus origami paper: 6 x 6 in., 54 sheets of rainbow-color paper.
ISBN: 0-87040-912-3

ORIGAMI CLASSROOM II by Dokuotei Nakano
Boxed set, board-book: 24 pp., 6 x 6 in., 24 pp. full color illustrations, plus origami paper: 6 x 6 in., 60 sheets of rainbow-color paper.
ISBN: 0-87040-913-1

ORIGAMI HEARTS by Francis Ow Mun Yin
120 pp., 7 1/4 x 10 1/4 in., 8 pp. color, 104 pp. line drawings, paperback.
ISBN: 0-87040-957-3

ORIGAMI MADE EASY by Kunihiko Kasahara
128 pp., 6 x 8 1/4 in., 113 pp. b/w photos and line drawings, paperback.
ISBN: 0-87040-253-6

ORIGAMI OMNIBUS: Paper-folding for Everybody by Kunihiko Kasahara
384 pp., 7 1/4 x 10 1/4 in., 8 pp. color, 360 pp. line drawings, paperback.
ISBN: 0-87040-699-X

ORIGAMI TREASURE CHEST by Keiji Kitamura
80 pp., 8 1/4 x 10 1/4 in., full color, paperback.
ISBN: 0-87040-868-2

PAPER MAGIC: Pop-up Paper Craft by Masahiro Chatani
92 pp., 7 1/4 x 10 1/4 in., 16 pp. color, 72 pp. b/w photos and line drawings, paperback.
ISBN: 0-87040-757-0

POP-UP BEST GREETING CARDS by Keiko Nakazawa
122 pp., 7 1/4 x 10 1/4 in., 16 pp. color, 102 pp. b/w photos and line drawings, paperback.
ISBN: 0-87040-964-6

POP-UP GIFT CARDS by Masahiro Chatani
80 pp., 7 1/4 x 10 1/4 in., 16 pp. color, 64 pp. b/w photos and line drawings, paperback.
ISBN: 0-87040-768-6

POP-UP GEOMETRIC ORIGAMI by Masahiro Chatani and Keiko Nakazawa
86 pp., 7 1/4 x 10 1/4 in., 16 pp. color, 64 pp. b/w photos and line drawings, paperback.
ISBN: 0-87040-943-3

POP-UP ORIGAMIC ARCHITECTURE by Masahiro Chatani
88 pp., 7 1/4 x 10 1/4 in., 4 pp. color, 11 pp. b/w photos, 68 pp. line drawings, paperback.
ISBN: 0-87040-656-6

Quick & Easy ORIGAMI by Toshie Takahama
Boxed set, book: 60 pp., 6 x 4 1/8 in., 30 pp. color and 30 pp. line drawings, origami paper: 3 packs in 6 colors (90 sheets).
ISBN: 0-87040-771-6

Quick & Easy FLYING ORIGAMI by Eiji Nakamura
Boxed set, book: 60 pp., 6 x 4 1/8 in., 30 pp. color and 30 pp. line drawings, origami paper: 3 packs in 6 colors (90 sheets).
ISBN: 0-87040-925-5

Quick & Easy ORIGAMI BOXES by Tomoko Fuse
Boxed set, book: 60 pp., 6 x 4 1/8 in., 30 pp. color and 30 pp. line drawings, origami paper: 3 packs in 6 colors (90 sheets).
ISBN: 0-87040-939-5

Quick & Easy ORIGAMI CHRISTMAS by Toshie Takahama
Boxed set, book: 60 pp., 6 x 4 1/8 in., 30 pp. color and 30 pp. line drawings, origami paper: 3 packs in 6 colors (90 sheets).
ISBN: 0-87040-870-4

TRICK ORIGAMI by Yoshihide Momotani
70 pp., 7 1/4 x 9 in., 4 pp. color, 56 pp. line drawings, 12 sheets of origami paper included, paperback.
ISBN: 0-87040-929-8

UNIT ORIGAMI: Multidimensional Transformations by Tomoko Fuse
244 pp., 7 1/4 x 10 1/4 in., 8 pp. color, 220 pp. b/w photos and line drawings, paperback.
ISBN: 0-87040-852-6

WORLD OF ORIGAMI, THE, by Isao Honda
182 pp., 8 1/4 x 11 3/4 in., 170 pp. b/w photos and line drawings, paperback.
ISBN: 0-87040-383-4